This book belongs to:

_____

Make A Wish

A *Faith 'n Stuff* Book

MARY LOU CARNEY

Fleming H. Revell Company
Tarrytown, New York

Acknowledgments

All scripture quotations, unless otherwise noted, are from the King James Version of the Bible.

Scripture verses marked (TLB) are taken from *The Living Bible*, copyright © 1971 owned by transfer to Illinois Marine Bank, N.A. (as trustee). Used by permission of Tyndale House Publishers, Wheaton, IL 60188.

Scripture verses marked (NIV) are from the Holy Bible, *New International Version*. Copyright © 1973, 1978, 1984 by International Bible Society. Used by permission of Zondervan Bible Publishers.

Excerpt on page 43 originally appeared in *Bible Knock-Knocks and Other Fun Stuff* by Mary Lou Carney. Text copyright © 1988 Mary Lou Carney. Used by permission of Abingdon Press.

"Special" by Mary Lou Carney is from *Pockets* magazine; September, 1986 published by The Upper Room, 1908 Grand Avenue, Nashville, TN 37202. Used by permission.

"Move the Paper Clip" trick from *Walter Gibson's Big Book of Magic For All Ages* by Walter Gibson. Copyright © 1980 by Walter Gibson. Reprinted with permission of Doubleday, a division of Bantam, Doubleday Dell Publishing Group, Inc.

"Dreams" from *The Dream Keeper and Other Poems*, by Langston Hughes. Copyright © 1932 by Alfred A. Knopf, Inc. and renewed 1960 by Langston Hughes. Reprinted by permission of Alfred A. Knopf, Inc.

Adaptation on page 61 is from "Up the Down Slope" by Adrienne Rivera which appeared in the March, 1988 issue of Guideposts magazine. Copyright © 1988 by Guideposts Associates, Inc., Carmel, NY 10512.

"Early Bird" from *Where The Sidewalk Ends* by Shel Silverstein. Copyright © 1974 by Evil Eye Music, Inc. Reprinted by permission of Harper & Row Publishers, Inc.

The cartoons appearing on pages 15 (bottom), 16 (bee, caterpillar), 23, 74, 85, 86, 88, and 123 are by Ron Wheeler from his book *Cartoon Clip Art for Youth Leaders* (Baker Book House). Used by permission.

The cartoons appearing on pages 15 (top), 29, 64, and 121 are from *Youth Specialties Clip Art Book Two*, copyright 1987 by Youth Specialties, Inc., 1224 Greenfield Dr., El Cajon, CA 92021. Used by permission.

The cartoons appearing on pages 16 (hippos) and 94 are reprinted from *Youth Ministry Clip Art*, copyright 1987, by Steve Adamson and Steve Hunt. The cartoons appearing on pages 36 and 100 are reprinted from *Outrageous Clip Art for Youth Ministry*, copyright 1988, illustrated by Rand Kruback. The cartoon on page 83 is reprinted from *Youth Ministry Clip Art Calendar*, copyright 1988. All published by Group Books, Box 411, Loveland, CO 80539.

Designed by Holly Johnson.
"Snappy Talks" and miscellaneous cartoons drawn by Stephen DeStefano.
Puzzles created by LMD Service for Publishers.
Printed in the United States of America.

ISBN 0-8007-5405-0

What's Inside?

Read Me First

Make A Wish! Have you ever watched the first star come out and made a secret wish? Or blown out your birthday candles while wishing for a new bike or roller skates? Wishes can be wonderful—especially when they come true!

For the next thirteen weeks, come share the adventures of kids a lot like you. Meet kids who go downhill skiing, dream of Olympic Games, struggle with their fears, and even write poems. Meet, too, a frog who was at the Red Sea Crossing during the time of Moses. And then there's Sammy—a little rabbit with a very *big* problem.

Meet Wally—a wise and witty snapping turtle. He's been waiting for a friend just like you! Check out his comic-strip adventure, "Snappy Talk."

During the coming weeks, you'll not only read God's amazing Word, you'll send your own messages to Him, too. Special calendar pages give you space to write in all those important events in your life—from soccer practice to birthday parties to book reports. Is there something about yourself you'd like to change or improve? Then check out "Building a Better Me." You might just learn how to make some of your wishes come true!

Remember, *Make A Wish* is your book. Write in the blanks, work the mazes, do the puzzles. You can even color the stars, if you want. Fun and faith, fascinating facts and new friends are waiting for you!

JANUARY

There once was a year sparkling new,
Just brimming with good things to do.
God wrapped it up tight
With rainbows so bright
And made it His present to *you!*

Have a GREAT New Year!

Did you know... January gets its name from the Latin word *jauna* meaning "door." So, get ready to open the door on a brand new year. It's going to be the best one you've had—ever!

1 New Year's Day _____   17 _____

2 _____   18 _____

3 _____   19 _____

4 _____   20 _____

5 _____   21 _____

6 Epiphany _____   22 _____

7 _____   23 _____

8 _____   24 _____

9 _____   25 _____

10 _____   26 _____

11 Banana Split Day _____   27 _____

12 _____   28 _____

13 _____   29 _____

14 _____   30 _____

15 Martin Luther King, Jr.'s Birthday _____   31 _____

16 _____

WEEK 1
Glad to Be Me

God's Amazing Word

> God saw all that he had made,
> and it was very good.
>
> Genesis 1:31 (NIV)

CHAMELEONS AND CURLS

For the tenth time, Mike parted his hair, trying to get his bangs to lie just right. "I hate the way I look!" he said into the mirror, throwing down the comb. "It's bad enough to have five zillion freckles. But these stupid curls make me look like a real baby!" He grabbed his books and ran down the steps to catch the school bus.

Gym class lasted forever. They played basketball, and Mike couldn't seem to make any baskets. Twice he double-dribbled the ball, and once he fell flat on his face when his shoe came untied. He was on his way to math when he heard his friend Gene calling him.

"Hey, Mike! Wait up. I've got something to show you." Mike stopped beside the drinking fountain. Gene hurried over and held out his stack of books. "Isn't it cool?"

Mike stared at the top book for a long time before he saw anything. Then he realized a lizard was resting there. A red lizard!

"It's a chameleon," Gene said. "It turns whatever color you lay it on. Let's put it on Mrs. Montag's desk and see what she does."

All day long the boys played with the chameleon. He turned green when he was on the plants at the back of the room and yellow when he was on the reading table. He even turned blue when they laid him on the back of Susie Perkin's blue sweater.

"I wish I could be like that chameleon," Mike thought to himself. "He always fits in. I feel like a real freak sometimes."

As they walked to the buses that afternoon, Gene said, "Hey, where's my chameleon?" Both boys began looking all around.

They finally found him inside Gene's jacket. "He's a hard one to find," Gene laughed. "I'd sure hate to be like him!"

"What do you mean?" Mike asked.

Gene shrugged. "It's just that he's always changing his color to fit in with everything around him. He's not like himself at all. It's almost like he's not even there." Gene waved as he got on the bus. "See you tomorrow."

Mike hurried to his bus, but all the way home he thought about what Gene had said. *He's so much like everything around him; he's not like himself at all.* Mike wanted to be like his friends, but he wanted to be himself, too. "So what if I can't dribble a basketball," Mike thought. "I got a really good grade on my science project." Just then he caught a glimpse of his reflection in the school bus window. And he smiled to see that his hair looked pretty good.

A Closer Look

Do you ever wish you were taller or bigger or thinner? Would you like to change the color of your hair or the size of your feet? That's only natural! Everybody wants to fit in, to be like everybody else. But we are each one a special creation—and part of what makes us special is that we are *unique.* Different from each other.

God loves variety, in nature and in people. He didn't cut out all the stars with a big cookie cutter. He made each one an original. He didn't make all flowers pink and all rocks gray. He made every part of creation to be special, different. And He did the same thing with His very best creation. You! So smile at yourself, and like yourself. God does!

What's Next?

Think about your best friend or favorite relative. What makes him or her different from other people? Maybe it's her sense of humor or the way he always listens when you want to talk. Whatever it is, why not tell that person how much you appreciate that unique quality? You could tell them at school or in a letter or even on the phone. But do it *soon*!

☆ ☆ ☆

Fun Stuff

Look at the animals below. In each row, several of them are just alike. But one is unique. Put an X on those that are alike. Circle the one that is different.

(See Answer Page.)

Those Amazing Animals!

Many animals have the ability to blend in with their environments: lizards and cheetahs and prairie squirrels and lots of others. One of the biggest animals that has this ability is the polar bear.

The polar bear's hair is not entirely white. Some of it is *transparent*. These transparent hairs reflect the colors around them. During the Arctic winters, the bears appear almost a bright white because of all the snow surrounding them. In the spring, when things begin to thaw, they appear yellowish because of the change in their environment.

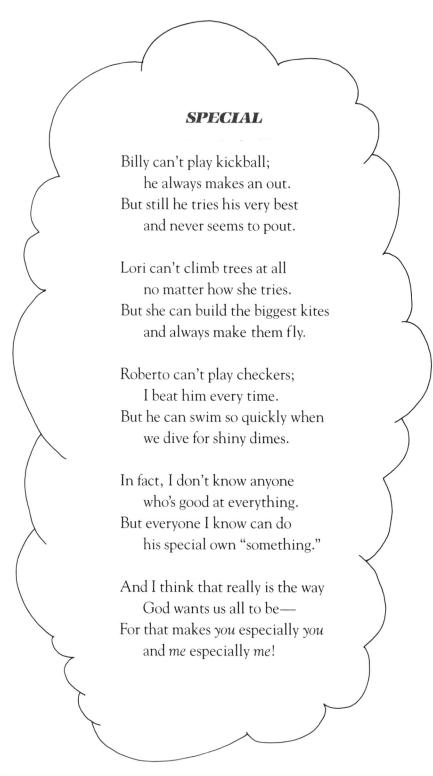

SPECIAL

Billy can't play kickball;
    he always makes an out.
But still he tries his very best
    and never seems to pout.

Lori can't climb trees at all
    no matter how she tries.
But she can build the biggest kites
    and always make them fly.

Roberto can't play checkers;
    I beat him every time.
But he can swim so quickly when
    we dive for shiny dimes.

In fact, I don't know anyone
    who's good at everything.
But everyone I know can do
    his special own "something."

And I think that really is the way
    God wants us all to be—
For that makes *you* especially *you*
    and *me* especially *me*!

Meet a Surprise Friend

Do you ever think about what you want to be when you grow up? Today there are so many choices, for both boys and girls. But when Elizabeth Blackwell was born in February 1821, there were certain careers women were not allowed to choose. And being a doctor was one of them.

But this did not stop Elizabeth. She wanted more than anything to help sick people. She was not allowed into medical school because only men could attend. So she studied on her own for three years. Finally she was admitted to Geneva Medical School. In 1853 she opened a special place to provide care and medicines for poor people in New York City. It was called a *dispensary* and was run entirely by women. Later she founded the Women's Medical College. Elizabeth used her special abilities to become the first American woman doctor.

From Me to God

You sure did a good job, God, creating neat stuff—plants and stars and beaches. And people. Thanks for making me unique. *Whenever I'm unhappy, I'm going to remember how special I am!*

WEEK 2
Spilled Milk and Special People

UDDERLY POSSIBLE

"But I've never even seen a cow close up, much less tried to milk one!" Shawn said as he and Jake walked through early morning darkness toward the barn.

"There's nothing to it," Jake said, unlatching the big wooden door. He and Shawn stepped inside and flipped on the light. In a nearby stall, something moved. "It's okay, Scarlet," Jake whispered, patting the back of the big, white-faced cow.

"Are you sure she won't kick me or anything?" Shawn asked as Jake got the bucket and stool from nearby pegs.

"Naw, not good ol' Scarlet. She's as gentle as a kitten. Just remember what I told you. Short, firm squeezes. And pull down gently on the teat each time. Watch me first." Jake pulled the stool near Scarlet. He talked softly to her as he sat down beside her bulging udder. "Got a lot of milk this morning, old girl." He reached for the two teats closest to him. Shawn watched, fascinated and scared at the same time. The only milk he'd ever seen came in cartons at the grocery, not from the lower side of a cow! Then suddenly a *ping-splash* echoed in the bucket. Then another. And another. A stream of steady white came from each tug Jake made. "Now, it's your turn," he said, sliding off the stool and motioning Shawn to take his place.

"No...I can't," Shawn protested. "I might...I don't know... hurt her or something."

"Come on!" Jake urged. "Just give it a try!"

Shawn sat down on the low stool. His knees were almost level with his chin. He tried to think of something to say to Scarlet. "Hi, there. We've never met, but I'm...well, I'm going to milk you." Jake laughed. Gingerly, Shawn reached for a teat. It felt warm and soft in his hand.

"Pull and squeeze," Jake prompted.

Shawn pulled. Scarlet shifted her weight and swished her tail against his back. "It's not working," he said.

"Squeeze as you pull. Just keep trying."

Shawn took a deep breath and tried again. *Ping-splash, ping-splash.* "I did it!" he said, grinning at Jake. "I can milk!" At that very moment, Scarlet gave a loud *moo.*

"That's Scarlet's way of saying, 'Don't quit now!'" Jake laughed.

"Right!" Shawn said, resting his head on Scarlet's side and filling the bucket with squirts of foamy, white milk.

A Closer Look

Have you ever been afraid to try something new? Everyone has! You may worry about looking silly or awkward. But people are meant to have new experiences, to try new things. Remember the first time you waded into the pool or tried to hit a baseball or played a C scale on the piano? It seemed strange and a little scary, didn't it? But soon you were diving for pennies and hitting home runs and playing real melodies.

You probably know that milk is important for bones and teeth. It helps you grow tall and strong. But did you know that you need to grow in other ways, too? Shawn was afraid to milk the cow because he'd never done it before. But once he tried it, he found out not only could he do it—it was actually *fun*! Part of growing is learning to face challenges, to push yourself to *try*. New experiences are God's special way of helping you do just that!

What's Next?

This month is the beginning of a new year, a year that will bring you lots of chances to try new things. Think right now of something you've been wanting to do, something you would like to learn more about. Maybe it's ballet or bow shooting, popping wheelies or playing Chopin. Whatever it is, this very week give it a try. Who knows, it might become your very favorite activity. Do it!

☆   ☆   ☆

Fun Stuff

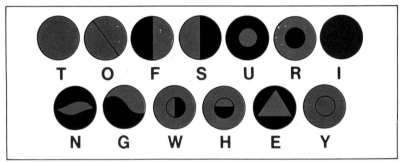

Key to code

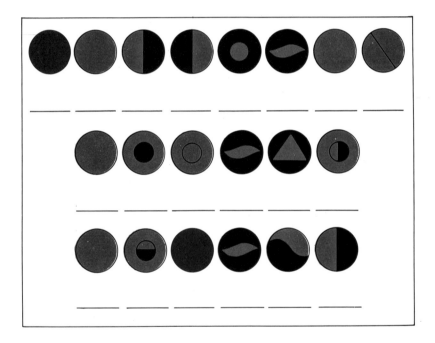

Use the code above to figure out this sentence:

— — , — — — — — — — — — —

— — — — — — — — — !

(See Answer Page.)

Meet a Surprise Friend

When Albert Schweitzer was a little boy, he always said his bedtime prayers. But he didn't think praying for people was the only important thing; he always prayed for animals, too. He loved animals—and people—all of his life. He became very famous for his kindnesses and great deeds all over the world.

Albert was born on January 14, 1875, in Alsace, a region on the French-German border. As a boy, he enjoyed playing the piano and making up games with his friends. When he grew up, he studied music and history and philosophy and religion. He was good at almost everything he tried!

But something made Albert unhappy. He knew that the world was filled with pain and suffering. He decided to do something about it. He became a missionary doctor. He and his nurse-wife Helene went to Africa. How glad the people were for the medicine and healing Albert brought them! There in the jungle they built a special hospital, one where families were allowed to come and stay with their sick ones. And in Albert's hospital, animals roamed freely around the grounds, like welcome friends. There was Parsifal, the pelican; Thekla, a tamed wild pig; Penci, a kitten; and Anita, a goat.

One of the greatest things about Albert Schweitzer was that he was willing to try all kinds of new experiences, to do almost any kind of work. In 1952 he was awarded the Nobel Peace Prize. Albert lived a long and wonderful life. He died in 1965, when he was ninety years old.

Tell Me Another One

On January 11, 1878, a milkman in Brooklyn, New York, delivered milk in glass bottles for the first time. Up until then, milk had been delivered in huge, metal cans. Each house had to provide its own container—a pitcher or a pail—for the fresh milk.

It was almost forty years later, in 1915, that Van Wormer invented throw-away paper containers that would hold milk. He

came up with the idea for paper cartons after dropping a full bottle in his toy factory in Toledo, Ohio. Milk went everywhere!

But it took Wormer almost ten years to invent a machine that would make the containers just right. Then many people who were used to the glass bottles didn't want to try the new paper containers. Finally, business picked up. By 1950, Van Wormer's company was producing the new containers at the rate of twenty million a day!

From Me to God

Thanks, God, for creating good things—like milk—that help me grow up tall and strong. But I want to grow in other ways, too. I want to know the joy of trying new things and having new experiences. With Your help, I'll be everything You want me to be. And I'll start this very day!

WEEK 3
Dreams Aren't for the Sleepy!

God's Amazing Word

> *Whatever you do,*
> *work at it with all your heart,*
> *as working for the Lord. . . .*
> Colossians 3:23 (NIV)

MUNCHIES AND GOLD MEDALS

"Come on, Carl," Jeff said over the blare of a television commercial. "This is getting boring!"

Carl took a long drink of his soda pop. "Boring? You must be kidding! The really good stuff comes on now, the old movies where gangsters carry machine guns and cops drive these funny cars."

28

"But we've been watching TV all day. Let's go outside and kick a ball around or something."

"Okay, okay," Carl said grumpily, flipping off the television and reaching for another candy bar.

The boys passed the soccer ball back and forth; they practiced their dribbling. "Let's see if we can find some of the other guys and get a game going," Jeff said.

Carl plopped down on the porch steps. "I'm pooped!" he said, wiping sweat from his forehead. "Let's just sit here for a while."

Jeff sat down, too. "So, what are you doing your oral report on? Mrs. Handlon says we have to have our ideas by Monday."

"The Olympics," Carl said. "I'm a real expert on the Olympics."

"Oh, yeah?" Jeff asked. "Why's that?"

"Because," Carl smiled confidently, "I'm going to be in them some day."

"The Olympics!" Jeff laughed. "You?"

"Yes, me," Carl said matter-of-factly.

"What event?"

"I haven't decided yet. Maybe the decathlon. I read this book about Bruce Jenner. He won that event for the U.S. in 1976." Carl tried to hold in his stomach and throw back his shoulders. "The decathlon takes a *real* athlete. Or maybe I'll be like Carl Lewis. In 1984 he won *four* gold medals." Carl stood up. "I'm going to go see if we've got any potato chips. Wanna come back in?"

Jeff shook his head. "I'm going to go find the guys and *do* something. Why don't you come along? Since you're going to be such a famous athlete," Jeff smirked, "maybe you could give us some pointers."

"You think you're smart, don't you?" Carl yelled as Jeff walked away. "I am so going to be in the Olympics! You just wait and see!"

"You'll be great if they add a 'couch potato' division. Or if there's a championship for who can eat the most junk food!" Jeff yelled back as he turned the corner and disappeared from sight.

"I'll show them," Carl said, rummaging in the refrigerator for the chip dip. "Someday I'll show them all...."

A Closer Look

Do you sometimes find that it's easier to talk about a thing than to do something about it? Talking about being a major league pitcher is more fun than running bases. Daydreaming about playing concerts in Carnegie Hall is more exciting than practicing scales.

Carl wants to be an Olympic champion. That's a great dream! But dreaming alone won't be enough to turn Carl from a chip-munching television addict into a tough, determined athlete. He needs to build muscles, to practice discipline, to learn to push himself. Even though he's still a kid, there are things Carl could be doing to help make his dream come true. Can you think of ways he might do this? Should he watch TV or join the school track team?

Dreams are wonderful things. They keep us reaching and planning. And, if we want them to come true, they keep us working, too!

What's Next?

Someone once said, "*Success* comes before *work* only in the dictionary." That's true, because all the *s* words come before the *w* words! But the saying is true in another way, too. No one can be successful in what he or she wants to do—whether it's running the high hurdles or discovering the cure for cancer or becoming president of the United States—without work.

Think right now of something you'd like to accomplish. Maybe it's something you want to do soon, like finishing a library book or weeding the garden or writing an overdue thank-you note. Or it could be a faraway goal, something you want to be when you grow up—a doctor, a teacher or an artist. . . . On the line below, write that one special thing you plan to do. Then, underneath it, write what you can do *today* to help make that dream come true.

_____

_____

Fun Stuff

Amy has a dream. Someday she'd like to be an...well, you can figure it out for yourself! Just shade in all the spaces below with a dot in them and find out what Amy wants to be.

(See Answer Page.)

Meet A Surprise Friend

Did you ever think about changing your name? That's exactly what Martin Lewis King Jr. did! When he grew up he changed his middle name to Luther because he was so impressed with Martin Luther, a great Protestant leader who lived hundreds of years ago.

Martin Luther King Jr. became a great leader himself. He went to college and became a minister. But he didn't just preach in churches on Sunday. He worked hard all week long trying to achieve equality for other black people. He became famous for his *nonviolent* way of dealing with situations. Dr. King did not believe in fighting, so he organized rallies where people got together to protest the way blacks were being treated. He also used sit-ins. During sit-ins, hundreds, sometimes thousands, of people would sit on sidewalks or in public buildings in an effort to get the problems of black people noticed. Dr. King won lots of awards for his efforts, including the Nobel Peace Prize.

But his work was cut short. On April 4, 1968, he was killed in Memphis, Tennessee. The whole United States was sad because of the death of this great man. His January birthday is now a national holiday.

Dr. Martin Luther King Jr.'s most famous speech was titled, "I Have a Dream." In it he talked about his dream of all people—of all colors—working and living together. Equally. In peace. Now that sounds like a dream we can all work for!

DREAMS

Hold fast to dreams
For if dreams die
Life is a broken-winged bird
That cannot fly.

Hold fast to dreams
For when dreams go
Life is a barren field
Frozen with snow.
—Langston Hughes

From Me to God

It's pretty neat, God, the way You gave me a mind that lets me dream about all the great things I'm going to do. Thanks for reminding me that I have to work now to make those dreams come true. Show me how to do that, Lord. Working together, You and I can make even the biggest dreams come true!

WEEK 4
Frogs and Faith

God's Amazing Word

As I was with Moses,
so I will be with you;
I will never leave you
or forsake you.

Joshua 1:5 (NIV)

DRY AS A FROG'S BELLY

"Tell us again, Grandpa Brutus. Tell us again!"

The old frog winked one of his huge eyes as the little frogs clustered around him. "It's gettin' where a body can't even take a nap in the sun without you young 'uns yappin' at him."

"But we want to hear about Moses and the Red Sea and all those chariots with iron wheels...." the littlest one piped up.

"All right, all right!" Grandpa said, swelling out his huge

body with a frog sigh. "I was just a little bit myself, not long hatched, when it all happened." The tiny frogs leaped closer. "It was an ordinary day at the Red Sea—a little log-sitting, a little fly-catching, a lot of croaking and hopping practice. Then, all of a sudden, a cloud of dust appeared on the horizon. A cloud made by the marching of thousands and thousands of humans. It came closer, and soon we could hear the bleating of their flocks and see the bright colors of their clothing. Now, most of the frogs skittered for cover. They didn't want to be the main course when these people sat down for dinner. But I...well, I was too little and stupid to know how dangerous human beings can be. So I just hopped up on a tree limb where I could see everything that happened. And plenty happened!"

"Is this the part about that wicked Pharaoh and all his army? About how they came after the people to make them slaves again in Egypt?" the littlest one asked.

Grandpa Brutus narrowed his eyes and glared. The tiny frog hopped behind his older brother. "As I was saying," Grandpa boomed, "plenty happened. I found out this swarm of people was the Israelites, and that God had just brought them out of years and years of slavery to the Egyptians. Their leader was a man named Moses, a man with a bushy beard and fiery eyes. Just as these Israelites reached the water, I saw another cloud of dust on the horizon. That's when the people started yelling and crying, 'It's Pharaoh! He's come to kill us. Weren't there enough graves in Egypt? Why did you bring us here to die in the wilderness?' But Moses stepped up on a rock and held up his staff. His voice shattered the desert stillness. 'Don't be afraid. The Lord will fight for you!'"

"Ooh...this is my favorite part!" the little frog croaked.

"And as the army got closer, a huge cloud came between the Israelites and the Egyptians. It was light on the Israelite side, but I could hear the army on the other side cursing and fumbling around in the dark. Then, Moses held out his rod over the Red Sea. A wind began to blow. Harder and harder. I wrapped my legs around the branch and stared down in disbelief. The water was splitting in two! A path of sand appeared smack in the middle of that great sea. Walls of water roared a hundred feet high. 'Cross over!' Moses commanded. And everyone did. All the people and animals. On dry ground. Incredible!"

"And when all the people were across, the cloud moved and Pharaoh tried it!" the littlest frog said, jumping up beside Grandpa. "But—*swoosh*—the walls of water came down and drowned all those Egyptians. *Glub! Glub! Glub!*"

"Whatever happened to Moses and the Israelites?" another frog asked.

Grandpa half-closed his eyes. "Word is that God took them to the Promised Land, helping them and feeding them all the way. Speaking of feeding...." Grandpa opened his eyes and, in a flash, his long tongue snapped at a fly. "Yummy," he said, patting his belly with a webbed foot. "And now for an afternoon nap."

The young frogs tiptoed off the log, and soon sounds of snoring echoed across the water.

A Closer Look

The Israelites had been slaves in Egypt for a very long time—almost three hundred years! God heard their prayers and sent Moses to help them. Moses was able to lead the people to freedom not because of his own strength or intelligence, but because of God's power. God is *omnipotent*, which means "all-powerful." He can do anything! He created the Red Sea, so He could control it.

God can control the situations in your everyday life, too. Bullies and best friends. Math tests and fights with your mom. Temptations to cheat and opportunities to be kind. As the Israelites did, you must pray for His help. Ask and believe!

What's Next?

Think now of something you have to do in the next few days, something that seems hard. Maybe even impossible. Perhaps it's a piano recital or a social studies project or a set of memory verses. It could be facing a kid who's been hassling you. Or even getting along with your brothers and sisters. Whatever it is, God can help! Read the verse below, taken from Philippians 4:13 (NIV).

"I can do everything through him who gives me strength."

Think about what this means. God is the One Who can give you the strength you need for anything and everything you have to do. Now, as you read the verse, make it your own by putting your name in the space provided.

"I, _____,
can do everything through Him (God) Who gives me strength."

(See Answer Page.)

Fun Stuff

Grandpa Brutus really loves eating flies! Can you help him catch this one? Grandpa has a message for you. Circle the *first* letter in the puzzle. Then, as you wind through the path after that sly fly, circle every *fourth* letter. Copy them in the blanks below. If you do a good job, you'll get some good advice and Grandpa will get his lunch!

___ ___ ___   ___ ___ ___ ___

___ ___ ___   ___ ___ ___

___ ___ ___ ___ ___ ___ !

Those Amazing Animals!

Frogs have been around for thousands of years. Before pollution and filling in ponds became common, frogs existed in huge numbers. History often talks about "plagues of frogs," times when great numbers of frogs would appear in fields and towns. In fact, one of the ways God persuaded Pharaoh to let the Israelites go was by sending plagues, or bad things, to Egypt. One of them was. . . well, you figure it out by solving this riddle. You can find the answer in Exodus 8:1-15.

> God sent plagues on Egypt.
> In all they numbered ten.
> Can you name the second one?
> It was totally, toadily grim!

(See Answer Page.)

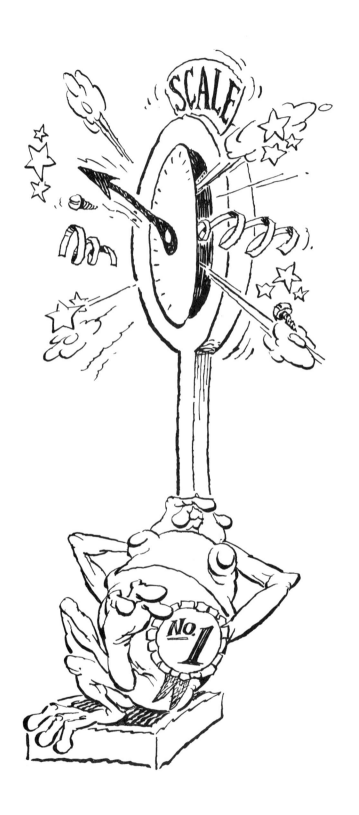

Tell Me Another One

Do you know how "Toad A" at the Blank Park Zoo in Des Moines, Iowa, became famous? He made his way into the *Guinness Book of World Records* as the world's *largest* toad! How large is he? He weighs 5 pounds, 1-1/2 ounces, measures 9-1/2 inches from nose to rump, and is 9-1/4 inches wide!

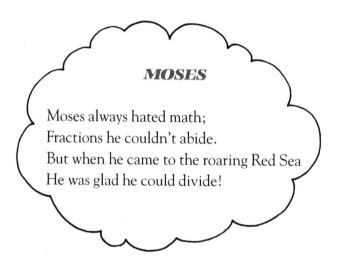

MOSES

Moses always hated math;
Fractions he couldn't abide.
But when he came to the roaring Red Sea
He was glad he could divide!

From Me to God

Wow, God, I wish I could have seen You part that Red Sea! Talk about awesome!

It's good to know that You can do anything—then and now. I'm going to remember that the next time I face something scary and hard.

Snappy Talk

Building a Better Me

How to Break a Bad Habit

1. *First ask yourself: What is it I want to do?* Stop biting my nails? Start turning in my homework on time? Keep my elbows off the table during dinner? Quit eating junk food in between meals? Whatever habit you don't like, promise yourself you'll change it.

2. *Work on breaking only* one *habit at a time, asking God to help you.* Like this:

> *Dear Father, I want to be everything You'd have me be. But I can't do it alone. I need Your help in breaking this habit:*
>
> _____ .

3. *Keep at it.* Habits are never easy to break. But just think... you'll soon feel happier and like yourself more. Maybe you'll even get along better with the kids at school, and more discipline might help you make the school track team or land a part in the class play or even be on the honor roll! Remember, whatever you want to accomplish—you can do it! And *don't give up!*

FEBRUARY

Knock, Knock.
Who's there?
Philip.
Philip who?
Philip these cold days
with warm thoughts!

Do you know why... February is the shortest month of the year? Thousands of years ago, Augustus Caesar, an emperor of Rome, took a day from February and added it to the month named after him. Can you guess what that month is? Right! It's August.

1 _____

2 Groundhog Day _____

3 _____

4 _____

5 Homerun King
Hank Aaron's Birthday _____

6 _____

7 _____

8 _____

9 _____

10 _____

11 _____

12 Abraham Lincoln's Birthday

13 First public school
in U.S. opened 1635

14 St. Valentine's Day _____

15 _____

16 _____

17 _____

18 _____

19 _____

20 _____

21 _____

22 George Washington's
Birthday _____

23 _____

24 _____

25 _____

26 _____

27 _____

28 _____

WEEK 5
Snow and Tell

God's Amazing Word

He [God] says to the snow,
'Fall on the earth'...
so that all men he has made
may know his work...

Job 37:6-7 (NIV)

SNOWBOUND SURPRISE

The wind whirled and moaned as it whipped falling snow against the window. Far down the road the twins saw the flashing lights of a snowplow.

"Why'd it have to snow today?" Janice groaned. "Now there's no way Mom can take us to the museum to see that dinosaur display."

"That's for sure," Jon said, turning away from the window and walking toward the fireplace. "It's even too cold for sledding."

Just then Mom came in with steaming cups of cocoa. "So, what do you two have planned for today?"

48

"Nothing," Janice said, poking at the marshmallows floating in her cocoa.

"Well," Mom said, "why not go exploring?"

"It's too cold outside!" Jon shivered.

"I mean inside," Mom smiled. "In the attic. There are lots of interesting things up there!"

After Mom left the room, Janice and Jon sat staring into the fire. Janice asked, "Think there's any neat stuff up in the attic?"

Jon shrugged. "It's worth a look, I guess."

The attic smelled of dust and dampness. Shadows played in the far corners, in places the light from the single bulb hanging overhead couldn't reach.

"It's kind of spooky," Janice whispered.

"It's just boxes and stuff," Jon said, his voice sounding loud against the low rafters. Slowly their eyes became used to the dim-

ness, and they could see things better. "There's my old dump truck," Jon said. "I thought Mom threw that out years ago. And here's Dad's footlocker from when he was in the Army!"

While Jon explored the trunk, Janice found a small box near the window. Gently she opened it and looked inside. "Love letters!" she gasped. "These must be Mom's old love letters!"

"Look at all these cool clothes," Jon said, pulling out a shirt with fancy patches and bright stripes on the sleeve. "They'd make great costumes for a play."

"Let's do it!" Janice said, holding the packet of letters in her hand. "Let's put on a play for Mom and Dad."

"All right!" Jon said, putting on a green cap with a shiny black bill.

The play was a great success. Jon spoke his lines like a truly brave officer, and Janice was lovely in a soft pink dress and matching hat. Afterward Mom and Dad clapped and clapped. The twins bowed and grinned and bowed some more. It hadn't been such a bad day after all!

A Closer Look

It's not always easy to be cheerful when your plans fall through. The twins really wanted to see that dinosaur display at the museum, and when the snowstorm came they thought their day was ruined. But it wasn't!

Have you ever watched young trees when a big storm comes? They seem to bend with the wind; they're *flexible*. *Flexible* is an important word for people, too. It means they're willing to change their plans, to try a different idea, to be creative instead of complaining. Remember that the next time you don't get your own way—about how you spend a Saturday or which restaurant your family eats at or where you sit in reading class. Be flexible! Like Jon and Janice, you may be surprised how much fun you'll have.

What's Next?

Can you make a paper snowflake? All you need is a square piece of white paper and a pair of scissors. Fold the paper in half diagonally, then in half two more times. Like this:

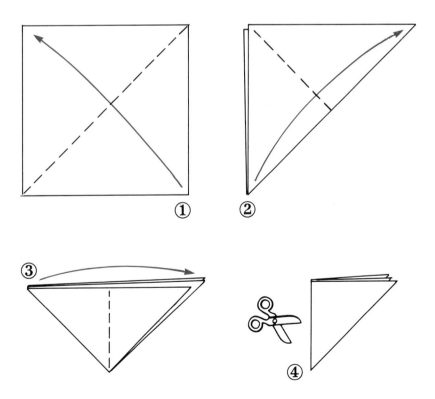

Begin cutting in some tiny shapes. *Snip, snip, snip!* Unfold it, and you'll have your very own snowflake.

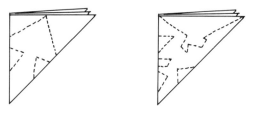

Why not send your snowflake through the mail and surprise a faraway relative or a good friend or even an elderly neighbor? (Be sure to get the correct address and a stamp.) Copy this poem on a piece of paper and include it:

> This fancy paper snowflake
> Is just my way to say
> I think you're pretty special—
> Have a wonderful winter day!

My Wonderful World

Did you ever wonder what snow's made of? Well, it may surprise you to know that those beautiful flakes begin as specks of dust! High, high up in the sky—about six miles or more—a drop of water in a cloud freezes around a speck of dust. Then that snow crystal begins falling to earth, changing all the time. By the time it lands outside your window, it's a beautiful work of art. And because God is such a special artist, no two snowflakes are alike!

Fun Stuff

Create your own snowflake by following the dots. Begin with number 1 and keep going until there are no more dots left to connect. *(But don't leave it in the sun—it might melt!)*

Wonderful Me!

Remember in the story how the twins couldn't see very well when they first entered the dim attic? But after a few minutes they were able to see much better. Do you know why?

Your eyes have a very special talent. The center of your eye, the tiny black circle inside the colored part, is called the *pupil*. The pupil is really a hole that lets light enter the eye so you can see. One set of muscles makes the pupil small when there is bright light, when you're at the beach on a sunny day or when your mom is taking pictures with a flash camera. Another set of muscles makes the pupil larger when the light is dim—when you're playing kick-the-can in the twilight or finding your way to the bathroom late at night. If you look in a mirror, sometimes you can actually see the center of your eye get smaller when you turn on a bright light. Your pupils stay busy all the time adjusting to the changing light around you.

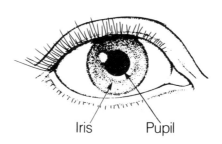

Iris   Pupil

Tell Me Another One

Would you believe that more snow falls in parts of Texas than at the South Pole? It's true! Although the South Pole is in Antarctica, the coldest place on earth, it gets only a few inches of snow each year. But that snow almost never melts. Instead it turns to tiny ice crystals. Over millions of years these crystals have covered the entire continent with ice.

From Me to God

It's pretty neat, God, how You can turn a speck of dust into something as beautiful as snow!

Sometimes when I don't get my way about things I . . . well, I don't act very nicely. I'm sorry about that, God. With Your help, I'm going to be more flexible.

WEEK 6
All in How You Look at It

God's Amazing Word

Now you are the body of Christ,
and each one of you
is a part of it.

I Corinthians 12:27 (NIV)

A SPECIAL FEELING

"Wow, that was a great story!" DeAnn said as she clicked off the tape machine.

"My mom gets them from the Society for the Blind. They even have recordings of most of the stories in our reading book. That really helps me since I can't see like the rest of you." Sharon felt on her bedside table for the tape case and handed it to DeAnn.

"What do you want to do now?" DeAnn asked.

56

"Let's go for a walk. I love the way the air feels after a fresh snow."

The two girls bundled up and started out the front door. Buster barked. "Not this time, boy," Sharon said, scratching his ears. "DeAnn will take good care of me." Sharon placed her hand lightly on DeAnn's arm as they started down the street.

The girls walked to the park. They scuffed their way through the tall snowdrifts on the baseball field. Then they played on the swings, squealing into the cold air as they pumped higher and higher. On the way back, they stopped at Molly's Café for hot chocolate.

"This feels good!" Sharon said, holding the warm cup between her hands. "But they forgot the marshmallows."

"Hey, you're right!" DeAnn said, staring into her cup. "How'd you know that?"

Sharon smiled. "I could tell by the smell. Marshmallows have a sweet, cotton-candy scent."

The girls finished their cocoa and were soon out in the cold crispness again. Just as they started to cross the street, Sharon stopped. "It's okay," DeAnn said. "The light's green."

"I think I hear an ambulance siren."

DeAnn listened. "I don't hear anything." Suddenly the scream of a siren broke the cold stillness. Soon an ambulance whipped around the corner and headed down the street for the hospital. "How could you hear that ambulance when it was so far away?" DeAnn asked.

Sharon grinned. "I don't know. My other senses seem to work harder trying to make up for my blindness. I can't see, but I sure can hear and smell and taste and feel!"

"Hey," DeAnn said as they crossed the street, "want to stop by my house and see my new sweater?" For a moment an awkward silence hung between the two girls. "Gosh, I'm sorry," DeAnn said. "I didn't really mean *see*, I meant..."

Sharon laughed. "I know what you meant. Let's stop by your house. I love new clothes. Besides," she said, tugging on DeAnn's jacket, "I have a real *feel* for fashion!"

A Closer Look

Have you ever known someone with a physical handicap or limitation? Perhaps there are classes in your school for children with hearing difficulties. You may have seen people with artificial arms or legs. Even ordinary things such as asthma and allergies can keep a child from running and playing like everyone else.

DeAnn and Sharon have a very special friendship. DeAnn helps Sharon "see" the world. Can you think of any way Sharon might help DeAnn? Perhaps she will make her more aware of sounds and smells, teach her to use more of her other four senses.

Even though disabled people can't do everything others can, they are still *people*—with likes and dislikes, dreams and fears, talents and ideas. Just like their non-handicapped friends!

What's Next?

Spend the next few weeks becoming aware of handicapped entries to buildings, of handicapped parking in lots. Do most stores think about these special customers? How about libraries and office buildings? You might want to write to the mayor of your city or to your representative in Congress, telling them how important it is to make sure disabled people can still shop and work, read and play in your city.

If you know someone who is handicapped, think now of something you can do to show your friendship. Maybe it's something as simple as a phone call or a game of UNO or a trip to the ice cream shop. Whatever it is, do it soon!

Tell Me Another One

Have you ever gone hiking in the woods? It's fun, isn't it, with all the neat things to see. But can you imagine a trail created especially for people who *can't* see? Well, just such a trail exists in a section of the George Washington National Forest in Virginia. Hikers follow a rope along the quarter-mile loop as they listen to birds, smell flowers, feel the bark of trees and wade through cold mountain streams. What if someone with sight wants to experience this "Braille trail"? Then he or she is given special dark goggles to wear.

Fun Stuff

It's the biggest basketball game of the season, and Biff doesn't want to be late. But he's having trouble guiding his wheelchair through all the obstacles—steps and curbs and escalators and such. Can you help him get to the gym?

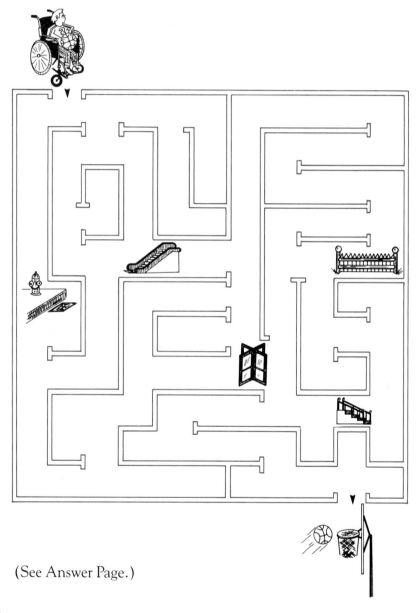

(See Answer Page.)

Meet a Surprise Friend

When Adrienne Rivera graduated from high school, she attended the University of Colorado. She swims and plays volleyball and climbs rocks and rides horses. What's so unusual about that? Adrienne has only one leg. When she was in the eighth grade she became sick with a rare form of cancer. In fact, only three people in a million get this disease. Adrienne had always been shy—embarrassed to talk in front of her class, afraid to go out for track, self-conscious about her thick glasses and her parents' divorce.

But after her leg was amputated, a strange thing happened. "Knowing how rare my disease was made me feel, well, *special*. I thought maybe God had chosen me somehow. And suddenly I got this terrific burst of courage!" That courage led her to talk to her class about her disease. It let her be part of a telethon for disabled children. It even sent her down a ski slope, wearing one ski and two outriggers—poles with little skis at the ends. "The second I went down that first bunny hill, I knew this was the sport for me," Adrienne laughs. And she was right. Adrienne now skis on the U.S. Disabled Ski Team.

Those Amazing Animals!

Some blind people have Seeing Eye dogs. These dogs are usually German shepherds or Labradors. Guide dogs were first used in Germany after World War I to help blind soldiers. A Seeing Eye dog has to be both smart and well trained. He learns to lead his master safely around obstacles and through traffic. Although the dog learns to obey commands, he will disobey them if obeying means putting his master in danger.

From Me to God

Thanks, God, for eyes to see and ears to hear and legs to run through snowdrifts on.

I know that handicapped people just want to be accepted. Help me to remember that the next time I have a chance to be a friend to someone with special limitations—and special talents.

WEEK 7
A Lot Like Love

God's Amazing Word

Let us not love with words...
but with actions....

I John 3:18 (NIV)

HAVE A HEART

"I can't wait until tomorrow!" Sarah said as they turned down the street toward their subdivision. "I just love Valentine's Day."

"Me, too," Tim said. "I hope every valentine I get is stuffed with candy."

"Do you have all your cards ready?" Sarah asked Becky.

Becky kicked at a stone on the sidewalk. "Just about. My mom says I have to give to everyone in my class this year."

"Even Nancy?" Tim asked.

Becky nodded. "Even Nancy."

"Yuck!" Sarah said. "She has the greasiest hair I've ever seen. And she smells!"

"I think that's because she's always sucking her thumb," Tim said, sticking his thumb in his mouth and sucking loudly. The girls giggled.

"Well," Becky said as she opened the gate into her yard, "I'm going to give her the one I like least!"

The reading table was covered with a red paper tablecloth. Cupcakes topped with tiny hearts were heaped on trays. Beside them stood rows of paper cups filled with pink punch. At the front of the room, the chalk rails were lined with brown bags decorated with cut-out hearts and lacy doilies.

"All right," the teacher smiled. "You may all go get your valentines now."

Laughing and scuffing, the class went forward. All except Nancy. "Don't you want to check your bag?" the teacher asked.

Nancy shook her head. "I know I didn't get anything. That's how it always is."

Becky hesitated as she started back to her seat. Then, she grabbed Nancy's bag off the ledge and dropped it on her desk as she went past.

Shyly, Nancy looked inside. One white envelope stared up at her. She opened it slowly, smiling as she tore the corners of the envelope. "Wow! It's beautiful!" she said, fingering the heart-shaped outline of the card. "Thanks, Becky. Thanks a lot! It's the prettiest valentine I ever got."

"Um...yeah...you're welcome." Becky watched Nancy sucking her thumb and reading—over and over—her one card. She looked at the pile of valentines on her own desk. "Hey, Nancy," she said, "you want to help me open some of these?"

"Sure!" Nancy said, taking her thumb out of her mouth and grinning.

Together the girls ripped open envelope after envelope. They read riddles and knock-knocks and funny rhymes. "This is the best Valentine's Day I ever had," Nancy said.

"Me, too," Becky smiled—and really meant it.

A Closer Look

Who do you think appreciated the gift of a valentine card more, Sarah who got twenty-three or Nancy who got only one?

It's easy to be nice to people who are nice to you, to someone who is pretty or smart or popular. It's not so easy to be nice to kids who always lose relay races or tattletale or are just different, somehow. But Valentine's Day is the perfect time to show *real* love—especially to someone who might need it. Why not try it? This could be *your* best Valentine's Day ever, too!

What's Next?

Make or buy a valentine card for someone who won't be expecting to receive one from you. Let it be someone from whom you don't expect to receive a card, either. Maybe your mailman or a faraway cousin or your pastor—or even your little sister. Surprise someone!

☆ ☆ ☆

Fun Stuff

Use the clues below and on the next page to fill in the Valentine's Day crossword puzzle.

Down:

1. February 14 is __ __ __ __ __ __ __ __ __'s Day.
2. On Valentine's Day you give your friend a __ __ __ __.
3. The color used most often in valentine decorations.

Across:

2. Sweet, sugary substance.

4. According to legend, Cupid shoots this to make people fall in love.

5. This is what Valentine's Day is all about, showing others you care about them.

6. Today is a good day to be ___ ___ ___ ___ to someone.

7. The shape used on valentines.

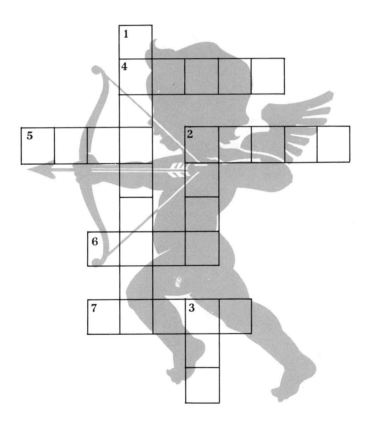

(See Answer Page.)

Can you count how many hearts are in the picture below? Make a *hearty* effort!

(See Answer Page.)

Tell Me Another One

Did you ever wonder why we celebrate Valentine's Day? Well, no one is sure how it all began. Some people think setting aside a day to celebrate love may have started back in ancient Rome thousands of years ago. The day probably got its name from a priest named Valentine. He lived seventeen hundred years ago, when Christianity was a new religion. He was put to death for teaching his beliefs and was later named a saint.

Wonderful Words

People all over the world spend today saying, "I love you." But how different it sounds in each country! Why not try your hand (tongue?) at saying these "familiar" words?

"I love you"	*Pronunciation*
French: *je t'aime*	jeh tem
Spanish: *Yo te amo*	yoh te A-moh
German: *Ich liebe dich*	eekh Lee-beh deekh

Meet a Surprise Friend

The year was 1847. Esther Howland received a lacy valentine from England. How beautiful it was! She had never seen anything like it in her hometown of Worcester, Massachusetts. So she decided to make some of these beautiful valentines and sell them in her father's store. Everyone loved Esther's work. Soon she was able to make a very good living—just from designing and making valentine cards!

From Me to God

Thanks, God, for Your love.
This week I'm going to show love to other people, especially people who are hard to love. But it's not going to be easy. Think You could help me? Thanks!

Snappy Talk

WEEK 8
On My Honor

God's Amazing Word

Have a clear conscience and desire
to live honorably in every way.
Hebrews 13:18 (NIV)

TROUBLE AT SCHOOL

"Hey, Abe! Come on 'fore you make us late." Nat Grigsby stood on the path in front of the Lincoln cabin. Ever since Abe's mother had died a few months before, the place had looked empty, somehow.

Abe came running down the path, his long legs sticking out from under his too-short trousers. "Mornin', Nat," he said. Abe looked much older than his nine years, and it wasn't just his height. There was something serious and sad about his face. "We'd better hurry. Schoolmaster Crawford will box our ears for sure if we're not in our seats and saying our numbers on time."

The two boys hurried down the path toward Pigeon Creek School, getting there just before Mr. Crawford arrived.

That's when the trouble began.

The room was full of children sitting on benches made of split logs. They talked quietly with one another, waiting for their teacher to appear. Suddenly, in a burst of good humor, Abe leaped up and grabbed hold of the deer antlers hanging above the door. "Look," he laughed. "I got me a deer by the horns...." But before he could finish, the antlers broke and Abe crashed to the floor.

Embarrassed, Abe made a dive for his seat just as the door opened and Mr. Crawford stepped into the room. The shattered pieces of deer antler lay at his feet. How proud he had been of those! They were his trophy from the only successful deer hunting he had ever done. His face reddened, and he reached for the switch on his desk. "Who," he thundered, "broke my deer antlers?" The room seemed to shake with the force of his question. No one spoke. "I'll find out who did it," he said, shaking the switch over the heads of the students in the first row, "if I have to punish every scholar in this room!"

Nat swallowed. He had been switched by Master Crawford before, and it hurt plenty! But he would never tell on his friend Abe. No one would. They would just take the whippings.

"I done it, sir." Abe stood with his head down. "I don't know why. Just all of a sudden I felt an urge to cut up and, well...I done it." He looked up into the cold eyes of his teacher. "But I'd never in a million years have done it if I'd thought they'd break."

A silence thick as March mud filled the room. Then Mr. Crawford's voice thundered again. "Get to work. All of you. I want to hear you do your spelling lessons good and loud now." He paused beside Abe's desk. "And you, Abe Lincoln, clean up that mess in front of the door."

"Yes, sir," Abe said, grabbing the weed-broom that stood in the corner.

Soon the room was noisy with the sounds of everyone studying his spelling out loud. Mr. Crawford looked pleased. The louder a "blab" school sounded, the more the students must be learning. He stepped close to Abe just as he finished sweeping. "Sometimes, boy, honesty may save you from a switching. But honesty's always the best strategy, even if it costs you a switching. Remember that."

"I will, sir," Abe said.

"Now, get to work," Master Crawford said in his usual strict voice. "Just because you're the best scholar in this room doesn't mean there's not a lot more you need to learn."

Abe skittered to his seat and grabbed the corner of the Blue-back Speller he shared with Nat. "H-o-n-e-s-t-y," he boomed in his best spelling voice. And for a second Abe thought he saw the beginnings of a smile on Mr. Crawford's face.

A Closer Look

Have you ever found yourself in a situation like Abe's in this story? It's hard to be a really honest person, always to tell the truth and take the blame for your mistakes. Sometimes you may be tempted to cheat on little things, to be less than truthful when no one will know. But little things aren't really so little when it comes to being honest: giving the cafeteria lady back that quarter-too-much she gives you in change; going straight to the office when the teacher sends you on an errand; not copying answers from someone else's homework; being truthful with your mom about where you go after school.

When Abraham Lincoln became president of the United States in 1861, he had a reputation for honesty. In fact, his nickname became "Honest Abe." Honesty in little things is essential to honesty in big things!

What's Next?

Below is a pledge, a promise to be honest always, even when no one else may know. Read it and think about it. Then, if you really want to be a person worthy of others' trust, sign your name on the line provided.

I promise, with God's help, to be truthful and to do what's right. I want to be an honest person—all the time!

_____

(your name)

My Wonderful World

Have you ever heard of Mt. Rushmore? It's a very special mountain in the Black Hills of South Dakota. The heads of four U.S. presidents have been carved into its side. Can you name any of them? Abraham Lincoln is one. The others are George Washington, Thomas Jefferson and Theodore Roosevelt. Their faces are almost seventy feet high.

Every year workers from the National Parks Service inspect these presidents to check for cracks. They also clean the sculptures. You may think your face gets dirty and hard to wash, but you should see these four! Workers must scrape plant growth and wasps' nests from the faces. Sometimes they even shoo away birds building nests in the huge eyes!

Fun Stuff

Below is some good advice—but first you'll have to figure out the secret code. Here's how. Look at each picture and decide what it is. Then write the first letter of that word in the blank below the picture. For example,

_____ _____ _____ _____ _____ _____

(See Answer Page.)

I Wonder Why?

Did you ever wonder why pictures of Abraham Lincoln always show him with a beard? A famous photographer named Matthew Brady made the first portrait of Lincoln. It was a very good picture, and Lincoln said later that he thought when people were able to see how he really looked, it helped him become president. In that picture, he didn't have a beard. But after he became president, an eleven-year-old girl named Grace Bedell told him that he would look better with a beard. In fact, she asked him if he would grow one. So...he did! Later, President Lincoln said he had grown the beard "in fulfillment of a little girl's wish."

Tell Me Another One

Abraham Lincoln had a unique way of saying things. He could use words to make people think about issues, like slavery and states' rights. But he could use words to make people laugh, too.

One day a man came to Lincoln and asked, "How long should a man's legs be?"

Lincoln looked first at the short man's little legs, then down at his own long ones. Slowly, he smiled. "Well," he said, "I reckon a man's legs ought to be long enough to reach the floor."

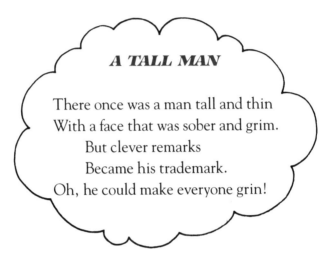

A TALL MAN

There once was a man tall and thin
With a face that was sober and grim.
But clever remarks
Became his trademark.
Oh, he could make everyone grin!

From Me to God

It's a relief to know that sometimes even famous people like Abraham Lincoln got in trouble at school!

I want to be honest, God. Really I do. But it's not easy. Help me, so that You can both be proud of what I do and who I am. Thanks.

Building a Better Me

How to Read the Bible

1. *Set aside a certain time each day to read.* Maybe it will be first thing in the morning, before you go to sleep at night or when you come home from school. Try to read the same time every day. Soon spending time with God's amazing Word will be a regular part of your day.

2. *Choose one book of the Bible and read in it for several days.* The Gospels of Matthew, Mark, Luke and John are good places to begin. You may find it easier to read a modern translation of the Bible: the New International Version, the Living Bible or the New King James.

3. *Pray that God will speak to you as you read His words.* The Bible has all the answers for your problems! It can help you make the right decisions, cheer you up when you're lonely, let you feel the closeness and wonder of God, and entertain you with some fantastic *true* stories. Most of all, the Bible can show you how you can become the person you really want to be. And that's Good News!

MARCH

EARLY BIRD

Oh, if you're a bird, be an early bird
And catch the worm for your breakfast plate.
If you're a bird, be an early early bird—
But if you're a worm, sleep late.

—Shel Silverstein

Wow! Isn't it great to have a month that's easy to spell?

1 _____

2 Dr. Seuss' Birthday _____

3 _____

4 _____

5 _____

6 _____

7 _____

8 _____

9 _____

10 _____

11 _____

12 _____

13 _____

14 _____

15 _____

16 _____

17 St. Patrick's Day _____

18 _____

19 _____

20 Spring Begins! _____

21 _____

22 _____

23 _____

24 _____

25 _____

26 _____

27 _____

28 _____

29 _____

30 U.S. bought Alaska
   from Russia in 1867 _____

31 _____

WEEK 9
Very Interesting!

God's Amazing Word

*There is a time for everything,
and a season for every activity
under heaven.*

Ecclesiastes 3:1 (NIV)

TO EACH HIS OWN

"Race you to the bottom!" Bart yelled, pushing off with his poles. His skis skimmed across the snow as he plunged toward the bottom of the hill, leaving the other skiers far behind. He came to a perfect stop just inches from the bench where Harold sat. He flipped the snow off his ski and onto Harold's coat. "When are you going to get off that bunny hill and have some real fun?" he teased.

Harold pulled his cap further down over his ears. "I don't know. Maybe never. The bunny hill's not so bad. I just like looking at the snow and watching everybody else. Did you ever notice how snow on the roof makes the ski lodge look like a gingerbread house? And when you fall in fresh snow, it smells like ice cubes...."

"When *you* fall in it," Bart corrected, turning toward the chair lift. "I don't fall. And I don't ski on baby hills, either." Harold watched as Bart made his way confidently through the lift line.

All day long both boys enjoyed the snow. Bart skied down the hill about a million times, weaving in and out of the slower skiers. Harold made a few trips down the bunny hill, but mostly he watched the other skiers or walked the wooded path along the side of the lodge. He listened to squirrels chattering and saw a big red cardinal.

It was almost dark when the two boys met again. "You sure ski good," Harold said.

"Yeah," Bart grinned. "I spend every Saturday here all winter. I love skiing better than anything." He looked down at Harold. "What'd you do all day?"

Harold shifted his feet. His boots made swooshing sounds in the snow. "Lots of things...."

"Like what?"

"Well...I...I wrote a poem. About skiing."

"No kidding?" Bart said with interest. "Can I see it?"

Harold reached in his backpack for his spiral. He opened it to the first page and handed Bart the notebook. It said:

> Snow bursts in my face
> like icy falling stars as
> I race down the hill.

"Wow! That's how it really feels, but I'd never have thought of it that way. You're pretty good with words," Bart said, punching Harold playfully on the shoulder. "Can I take this poem home with me? Then I can read it anytime I want and remember what it feels like to burn down the slope."

"Sure," Harold grinned, tearing out the page and handing it to Bart.

Then, together, the two boys headed for the lodge and some steaming cups of hot cocoa.

A Closer Look

Can you imagine how boring the world would be if everyone looked alike and dressed alike and did everything just alike? No two snowflakes are just the same, and no two people should be, either. It's okay to enjoy different things! There's no "right" and "wrong" when it comes to hobbies or sports or other interests. In fact, we can learn a lot from each other. So be yourself—and share yourself!

What's Next?

Do you know someone who has an unusual interest? Maybe it's rock collecting or needlepoint or indoor gardening. Perhaps it's creating collages or playing rugby or building models. Take time soon to ask him or her about it. Who knows—you may find a whole new interest of your own!

☆   ☆   ☆

Fun Stuff

Have you ever heard of *haiku*? It's a special form of poetry borrowed from the Japanese. Each haiku poem has three lines and creates a special "picture" of nature. But what makes haiku such fun to write is that each line contains a certain number of syllables: line one has five syllables; line two has seven; line three has five. With haiku, you don't have to worry about rhyme. You just count syllables and create pictures! Use your imagination to see what is happening in this haiku.

> My shadow shivers
> on freshly frozen snowbanks:
> February walk.

Go back now and read Harold's poem in the story. Count the syllables in each line. Is it a haiku? That's right, it is!

Now, in the space below, try writing your own poem. Think of something in nature you really like. Maybe it's a summer sunset or a green frog sitting on a slimy log or crystal icicles or spring's first tulip. Paint a word picture of the scene using three lines. Or you may want to make your poem a haiku. If you do, the words you choose should equal five syllables in the first line, seven syllables in the second line and five syllables in the last line.

MY POEM

_____

_____

_____

Tell Me Another One

Some Februarys have twenty-eight days while others have twenty-nine! That's because the true solar year is really several hours longer than 365 days. To make up the difference, "Leap Year" was introduced. Every fourth year February gets an extra day, except in "century" years not divisible by four hundred. So 1900 wasn't a leap year. Will 2000 be one?

(See Answer Page.)

Meet a Surprise Friend

Robert Frost is one of the most famous of all American poets. He was born in San Francisco, California, in 1874. He liked to write about country things: snowy woods and hoeing corn and mending fences. He believed that poets should write the way people talked. On his eighty-eighth birthday, Mr. Frost was awarded the Congressional Medal at the White House. The United States Post Office even issued a commemorative stamp in his honor! Robert Frost died in 1963. You may want to look in your local library for some of his books, especially *You Come, Too.*

I Wonder Why?

Did you ever wonder why a ski jumper leans forward on jumps? It's because he's pretending he's an airplane wing! In order to go farther, ski jumpers imitate the shape of airplane wings:

rounded in front, curved on top, and flat on the bottom. So skiers tilt their skis up and lean forward. Air rushes over their curved backs, producing less pressure. When air pressure above a skier is less than air pressure below him, he is able to lift higher and jump farther. To almost *fly*!

Wonderful Words

Do you have a special hobby, something you like to do in your spare time? The word *hobby* comes from a word meaning "little horse" or "toy horse." Now everyone knows a toy horse is just for play—he can't be made to drag a plow or jump a hedge or even pull a wagon. So the word *hobby* came to mean something that's not work. A hobby is something you do just for *fun*!

From Me to God

I'm glad You didn't make a boring world, God. There's so much to see and do! And I really like the way You let different people be good at different things. That way we have a lot to share with each other. Thanks!

WEEK 10
Furry Friends and More

God's Amazing Word

For the Lord grants wisdom!
. . . He shows how to distinguish
right from wrong, how to find
the right decision every time.

Proverbs 2:6, 9 (TLB)

REGGIE'S CLOSE CALL

B.J. pushed hard on the round, white doorbell. From inside echoed the familiar *ding-dong*. Mrs. Whiting opened the door. "You're right on time," she smiled. "And Reggie is all ready." B.J. stepped inside while Mrs. Whiting snapped the leash on Reggie's fancy red collar. Reggie yapped and twisted with excitement.

90

"He so enjoys these walks, and my arthritis has been acting up lately." She handed B.J. the leash. "Now remember, you can't be too careful."

"Yes, ma'am," B.J. said as he and the dog started down the steps. He had been walking Reggie every afternoon after school for the last two weeks, and Mrs. Whiting always said the same thing. B.J. turned down the sidewalk, thinking about what he would buy with the money he was earning.

Reggie pulled and tugged on the leash. He wanted to sniff every leaf, explore every walk. "This way," B.J. laughed, pulling him toward the park. Once in the park, B.J. ran with Reggie—around in big circles with the leash like a long piece of licorice joining them. B.J. stopped to catch his breath, but Reggie wanted to play. He kept wrapping the leash around B.J.'s legs. "Cut it out!" B.J. laughed, tripping as he tried to untangle himself. "I wish I could take this dumb leash off you for a while and let you really run. I bet I could teach you to fetch a stick in no time!" Reggie wagged his tail.

B.J. looked around the park. Almost no one was there—just a few kids way over on the swings. "How about it, boy?" B.J.

asked, picking up a nearby stick and holding it in his hand. "Want to learn to fetch?" Reggie barked and pranced around on his hind legs. "Okay. But just for a few minutes." B.J. reached for the silver clasp and undid the leash. "Go get it, boy!" he yelled, throwing the stick with all his might. In a flash of fur and running legs, Reggie took off after it. But he didn't stop when he came to the stick. Instead, he kept on running—right toward the street! "Reggie!" B.J. yelled, racing after him. "Come back!"

The screech of tires sounded in B.J.'s ears like a million fingernails run across the chalkboard. "Reggie!" he screamed. Traffic stopped. Reggie turned toward B.J. The big dog looked scared and confused there in the middle of the street. "Here, boy," B.J. said softly. "Come here." Just then a dump truck blew its horn. Reggie bounded back to the sidewalk. B.J. threw his arms around Reggie's neck and snapped the leash in place. "Bad dog," he scolded. "Why did you run into the street like that? Bad, stupid dog!"

But as they walked toward home, B.J. knew it wasn't Reggie's fault that he'd almost gotten hit by a car. It was B.J.'s. "I should've kept you on the leash," he mumbled. "I just wanted you to have some fun. I never thought you might get hurt or anything." As they turned into the yard, B.J. knelt down to scratch Reggie's ears. "I guess Mrs. Whiting is right. You *can't* be too careful. And I'll never forget that again!"

A Closer Look

Did you ever take a tiny snowball and begin rolling it around in the snow until finally it got so big you could hardly budge it? Other things work that way, too. It has to do with *consequences*.

Consequences are the results of things we do and decisions we make. If you don't do your homework, you may get in trouble at school. Staying up late may keep you from playing your best in the big soccer game. Junk food fills your body with empty, useless calories.

But not all consequences are *bad*. Obeying rules and being kind and planning ahead can all have *good* consequences. If you make the right choices, consequences can be great!

Letting Reggie run without his leash didn't seem like a big deal to B.J.—but it almost had tragic consequences. It's important to learn to *think* before you act.

What's Next?

Part of living together in a family is sharing work. Think now of some particular responsibility you have. Maybe it's feeding the cat or making your bed or taking out the trash or practicing your clarinet. Do you ever have trouble making yourself finish your work? Not doing chores may have bad consequences!

On the line below, write down a particular chore you must do.

A job I must do is:

_____

Now, write what you can do to help you make sure that the job gets done *right*. Perhaps you could list the task in your school assignment notebook or write it on your *Faith 'n Stuff* calendar page. Could you finish your chores before watching television? Or how about a reminder on your mirror?

Things I can do to make sure my chore gets done:

_____

_____

☆   ☆   ☆

Fun Stuff

Here's a fun activity to help you think about consequences. In the first column are several decisions; in the second are the consequences. Draw a line from an action in the first list to its consequence in the second. The first one has been done to show you how. And remember, you can't be too careful!

Practices piano every day — Falls asleep during morning reading class

Stays up late on school night

Bad stomachache!

Forgets to feed the dog

Good checkup at dentist

Lies to Mom about where she went after school

Pet goes hungry

Eats a whole bag of choco-late-covered peanuts

Does well at recital

Drinks plenty of milk

Feels miserable; Mom finds out and punishes

Riddle

Knock, knock.
Who's there?
Howl.
Howl who?
Howl I avoid bad consequences?

Cross out every third letter below for the answer!

Treusot isn tbhe zLomrd banqd dko gwoosd....

(Psalm 37:3)

(See Answer Page.)

Those Amazing Animals!

Have you ever seen a St. Bernard? What huge, hairy dogs they are! St. Bernards are famous for the lifesaving work they do in cold, snowy climates.

St. Bernards never lose their sense of direction, no matter how bad the storms get or how far away from home they are. This built-in radar also lets them know where victims are buried in the snow. Then the great animals rush over and begin digging.

The most famous St. Bernard of all was Barry. In the early years of the nineteenth century, he braved snow and ice and wind to find victims trapped beneath avalanches or lost on unfamiliar trails. Between 1800 and 1814, he saved the lives of more than forty people!

Tell Me Another One

Laika, an Asian spitz, was the first dog to travel into space. She was launched by the U.S.S.R. on November 4, 1957. For ten days she orbited the earth, sending back vital information that would later allow *people* to make the fantastic trip.

From Me to God

I'm glad You created dogs, God. They sure make good friends! It's sort of scary to think that everything I do has consequences. Could You help me make good decisions so the consequences will be good, too? Thanks!

WEEK 11
Magic All Around Me

God's Amazing Word

Give thanks to the Lord of lords...
to him who alone does great wonders....
Psalm 136:3–4 (NIV)

ABRA-CA-DA-BRA!

"And now, the Marvelous Martini must be off to other adventures!" The magician stuffed the gray scarf into a hollow tube as he talked. Then, magically, he pulled a brightly colored scarf from the other end. Blue and yellow and red and purple. He waved the scarf at the bleachers of children and took a deep bow. Everyone clapped until his hands hurt.

"That was some assembly!" Susie said when they were all back in the classroom. "Didn't you just love all his tricks?"

"Especially the one where he made the rabbit disappear," Carrie added.

"I'd have liked it better if he'd have made Mr. Allen disappear," Fred laughed.

Just then Mr. Allen walked in. "How many of you enjoyed the magic show?" he asked. Every hand in the room went up. "You know, there's all kinds of magic. Black magic and white magic—and green magic."

"*Green* magic?" Susie said. "What kind of magic is that?"

Mr. Allen smiled. "I was hoping you'd ask." He went to the back of the room and brought out a tray of tiny, green sprouts. "These are lima beans that have been placed on wet paper towels."

"Probably cafeteria rejects," Fred whispered.

Mr. Allen pretended not to hear. "And now we're going to do a little 'green magic' of our own."

Soon all the students were busy filling small white cups with dirt. Then, carefully, they each pushed a bean sprout beneath the soil. They initialed their cups and placed them in a sunny window beside the reading table.

"What's so magical about a muddy thumb?" Fred asked as he rinsed his hands.

"Just wait," Mr. Allen said. "We'll keep the soil moist and say 'abra-ca-da-bra' every day. Soon you'll all be magicians!"

Sure enough, in just a few days tiny plants began appearing.

"Look at mine!" Susie said, holding her cup gently.

Fred stared into his cup of dirt. Nothing. "Hey," he said, "how come I don't have a plant like everybody else?"

Mr. Allen looked very serious. "Maybe you didn't say the magic word loudly enough, Fred."

"Ah, come on. What difference would that make?"

"Green magic is a very special thing. Perhaps if you'll close your eyes and say the magic word, it will help."

Fred looked at all the other plants, green and growing in the sunlight. He looked at his empty cup. "Guess it can't hurt," he shrugged. He closed his eyes. "Abra-ca-da-bra!" he shouted.

Quickly, Mr. Allen replaced Fred's cup with one he had behind his desk. A healthy bean sprout stuck up from the soil. When Fred opened his eyes, he could scarcely believe it.

"Wow! That was quick!" Fred said. "Just imagine how big it would've got if I'd really screamed the magic word."

"Yes," Mr. Allen winked at the rest of the class. "Just imagine!"

A Closer Look

The "wonders" of magicians are really very clever tricks. They work hard at the art of illusion. But God has put lots of real wonders around us, amazing things we hardly even notice: grass that turns green every spring; a baby's tiny fingers; rivers that run to the sea; stars that stay in their constellations. The fact that these things happen so often makes them even *more* wonder-full!

What's Next?

God's own special magic is all around you. Open your eyes and search, this very day, for some "wonder" you may not have really noticed before. Perhaps it's bread rising or the sun setting or a flower blooming. But keep looking until you find it. Then share your discovery with a parent or close friend. *Abra-ca-da-bra*—begin!

☆　　☆　　☆

Fun Stuff

Below is a secret message just for you. Having trouble reading it? Hold this page up to a mirror, and the correct message will magically appear!

How would you like to learn a magic trick? You can amaze your friends with this "Move the Clips" trick.

Lay several paper clips in a row on the table. Ask somebody to move some clips one by one from one end of the row to the other. Tell them they must move the clips from right to left. Have them do this while you turn your back or leave the room. When you come back to the table and just pass your hand over them, you immediately name the number moved.

Magic, right? Well... not quite.

One clip gives you the clue. It is at the right end of the row. This last right-end clip is placed so that its long end is opposite those of the others—a detail that no one notices. After the clips are moved you simply count from the left end of the row, including the inverted clip. And—ta-da!—you are able to tell your friends the number moved.

These pictures will show you how the trick is done.

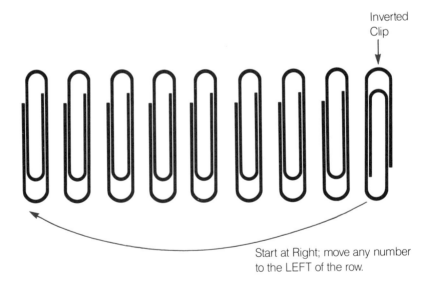

Inverted Clip

Start at Right; move any number to the LEFT of the row.

Suppose your friend moved five clips. It would look like this.

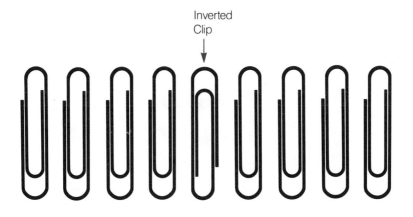

Inverted
Clip

Meet a Surprise Friend

What do you think of when you hear the word *green*? During the month of March, most people think of St. Patrick's Day. St. Patrick was a real person who lived in the fourth century. He was a missionary to Ireland, converting this "emerald isle" to Christianity. Legend claims he used a shamrock to explain the Trinity.

Wonderful Me

Do you remember your first haircut? You may have been afraid it would hurt. After all, that's part of you! But *snip-snip*...magic! It didn't hurt at all. Do you know why?

Hair is made of two major parts, the shaft and the root. The shaft is the part you comb—and cut. It's made up of old cells, just

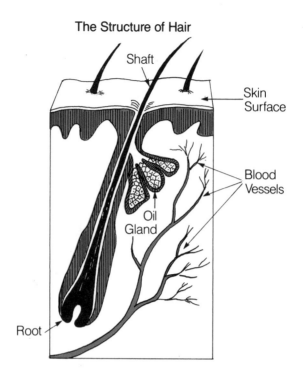

The Structure of Hair

Shaft

Skin Surface

Blood Vessels

Oil Gland

Root

like your fingernails and toenails are. The root, however, is live cells. That's why it hurts when someone pulls your hair. But cutting your hair doesn't hurt, because the scissors are only clipping off dead cells.

From Me to God

Thanks, God, for all the wonders You placed right here in front of me. You're the best magician of all!

Snappy Talk

WEEK 12
Band-Aids and Best Friends

God's Amazing Word

Be kind and compassionate
to one another,
forgiving each other, just as in Christ
God forgave you.

Ephesians 4:32 (NIV)

CAFETERIA CLASH

Mark kicked his locker shut. He took one more look down the empty hallway. Jason was nowhere around. "Who cares!" he said aloud, heading toward the door.

108

Halfway home Mark caught up with his little sister Lorie. "Where's Jason?" she asked.

"On some other planet, I hope!"

Lorie looked at Mark. "That's a weird thing to say about your best friend."

"He's not my best friend! Not after today."

"What happened today?"

"It was during lunch. Jason and I were in line, getting our food. We'd just started toward a table when this little kid comes tearing out of nowhere and rams right into me. My tray flew up in the air, and food went everywhere!"

"How embarrassing!"

"Yeah, I kept wishing I were invisible! At first the cafeteria was so quiet you could almost hear the milk running down the front of my shirt. Then somebody laughed, and the whole place started clapping and yelling 'Way to go!' and 'Hey, Clumsy!' and stuff like that."

"Where was Jason?"

"That's what makes me so mad. He went to sit with some other guys and just left me there, scraping food off the floor." Mark frowned. "I didn't talk to him the rest of the day. And it would suit me fine if I never had to see his ugly face again!"

Just as Mark and Lorie started up the front sidewalk, they heard the phone ringing inside their house. Mom pushed open the door. "Telephone, Mark. Hurry! It's Jason, and he says it's important."

But Mark didn't hurry. Instead, he stood there on the sidewalk, feeling the knot of anger tighten inside his stomach.

A Closer Look

It's fun having a best friend, isn't it? Someone to go bike riding with and tell special secrets to. Someone to help you with your science project and sleep over on Friday nights. But when that special friend lets you down, you can feel pretty rotten. The way Mark is feeling now. And it's the kind of "inside" hurt that a Band-Aid can't help.

Why do you suppose Jason didn't stay and help Mark pick up his tray? Was it because he suddenly stopped liking Mark and wanted to be mean to him? Or was it because he wished he could be invisible, too? Maybe Jason just wanted to get as far away from the situation as possible.

It's important to be a good "forgiver." When you forgive someone, you don't hold a grudge, you don't keep remembering his mistakes, you don't try to make him feel miserable for what he's done. It's even important to forgive *yourself* sometimes, when you mess up an assignment or forget to do a chore or even do something you know is wrong.

The very best forgiver of all is God. Even though He never goofs up or makes mistakes, He is willing to forgive us imperfect, fumbling people! Now isn't that a relief?

What's Next?

Why do friends let you down? Sometimes it's because they're embarrassed by something that happens—as Jason was when Mark dropped his tray in the cafeteria. Or it could be because they're trying to impress someone new.

But friendship works two ways. Part of what will make you a

good friend is being able to forgive someone who does something that hurts you. Even if it hurts you a lot. *Especially* if it hurts you a lot.

What do you suppose happens to Mark and Jason? Do they stay best friends? Do they have a fight? Does something embarrassing happen to Jason? If so, what does Mark do? Does Jason apologize to Mark? Does Mark forgive him? Draw in the box below what happens at school the next day.

Fun Stuff

Have you ever heard of a section near the back of the newspaper called the Classified Ads? Here people advertise things they have for sale, everything from boats to beagles. But some people also run ads looking for specific things—a rare coin, help with their yard work, a part-time housekeeper. In the space below, write your own classified ad. What are you looking for in a best friend? Honesty? Good looks? Cool clothes? A sense of humor? Be specific.

```
            WANTED! BEST FRIEND!

        He or she must meet these
            qualifications:

    My best friend must _____

    _____

    _____

    _____
```

Now that you're all finished, go back and read the ad. Pretend someone else wrote and placed it in the newspaper. Could you answer the ad and be the Best Friend they're looking for? Do you have all the qualities you expect in someone else? Remember, the best way to *have* a friend is to *be* a friend!

Wonderful Words

Can you decode this secret word? It's something every friend must be able to do. To get the answer, just write the letter of the alphabet that comes *before* the one given.

<u>g</u>   <u>p</u>   <u>s</u>   <u>h</u>   <u>j</u>   <u>w</u>   <u>f</u>

___   ___   ___   ___   ___   ___   ___

(See Answer Page.)

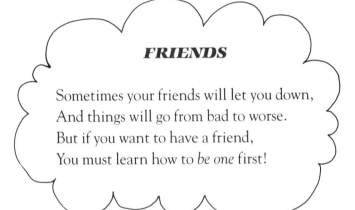

FRIENDS

Sometimes your friends will let you down,
And things will go from bad to worse.
But if you want to have a friend,
You must learn how to *be one* first!

Wonderful Me

Whenever you wreck your bike or fall out of a tree or trip going up your back steps, you can injure some of your skin. But your body has the ability to replace that damaged skin. Here's how:

Skin is made of two parts: the epidermis and the dermis. The epidermis is the outer part, made up of cells that are almost all

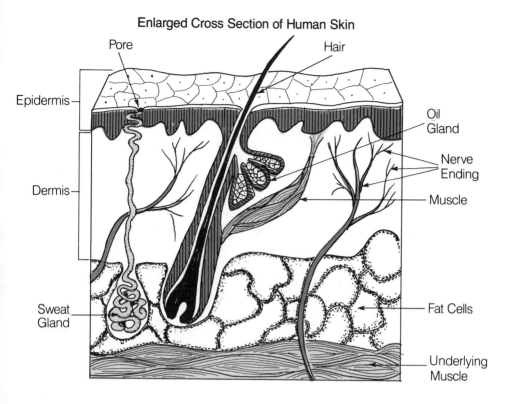

Enlarged Cross Section of Human Skin

dead. The dermis, however, is made of living cells—cells that are continually multiplying. As they multiply, they push up the older cells. Soon your cuts and skinned places are covered by a new layer of these cells. A new epidermis is created!

Meet a Surprise Friend

Mr. Dickson's new bride Josephine was accident-prone, always cutting or nicking or scraping herself. But because he worked for a company named Johnson & Johnson that made gauze and adhesive tape, Mr. Dickson knew just what to do. He cut tape into strips and stuck a little square of gauze in the middle of each strip. Now, whenever Josephine had an accident, her bandages were waiting.

Johnson & Johnson heard about these bandages that were both quick and easy to apply. And in 1924 they installed machines to make the new product. The Band-Aid was born!

From Me to God

Thanks, God, for loving me even when I mess up. And for being such a good forgiver. I'm going to work hard to forgive other people, too. Even the ones who don't say, "I'm sorry."

WEEK 13
A Little Lesson

God's Amazing Word

> I have learned to be content
> whatever the circumstances....
>
> Philippians 4:11 (NIV)

SAMMY'S WISH

Sammy sat on the edge of the pond, staring at his reflection. "What a wimpy, shrimpy rabbit you are!" he said to himself.

"You'll have to speak up, young 'un. My ears ain't what they once was." Old Abner stretched and crawled toward Sammy. He was the oldest snail in the hollow, and the wisest, too.

"I wasn't talking to you. I was talking to myself," Sammy said, kicking a pebble into the water and watching his reflection disappear into ripples.

"*Humph.* Sounds like a pretty one-sided conversation to me." Abner peered through his thick glasses at Sammy. "You look mighty unhappy for such a little guy."

"That's exactly *why* I'm unhappy!" Sammy yelled. "I'm so small! I'm tired of being the littlest one in the family and the scrawny one in all the games. I wish I were big, big, big!"

"Better be careful with those wishes," Abner whispered, inching closer. "It's twilight in the hollow—the time of magic and mystery, when some wishes are best left unsaid."

"I'll say it again and again and again." Sammy stood up on his rock and shouted at the sky. "I want to be big, big, *big!*"

The sky darkened a bit. A thick silence filled up the hollow. Then a wild wind began blowing in off the pond. "I'd best be getting back," Abner said, tucking his chin against his shell as he faced into the wind. "And you'd better run home, too."

"I'm not going home," Sammy called after him. "I'm going to wait here until my wish comes true. Until I'm *big*." He leaned against the trunk of the tree and yawned. "I'll wait forever if I have to...."

When Sammy opened his eyes, shafts of sunlight surrounded the pond. He leaned over to look at his reflection in the water. A giant rabbit looked up. Sammy jumped back, frightened. Slowly, he leaned forward again. "Is that really me?" he wondered aloud. "Am I really that big?"

He looked at the swamp around him. How small everything looked! It was as if the trees had shrunk to the size of sunflowers. And the big rock he always sat on now felt as small as an Easter egg. "I'm big!" Sammy laughed, jumping up and down until the ground shook. "Wait till I show my family!"

Sammy raced toward the familiar hole leading to his cozy home beneath the ground. But he was much too big to fit through the small opening. "Oh, no!" he said, sitting back on his giant haunches to think. But before he could figure out what to do, his friend Shirley Squirrel came scurrying by. "Hey, Shirley, notice anything different?" Sammy grinned.

"Wel-l-l, you have certainly grown!" she gasped.

"Can I play with the rest of you now?"

"I guess so," she said slowly.

How excited Sammy was finally to be a part of the fun! But things didn't work out quite the way he thought they would. He was too big to find a hiding place when they played hide-and-seek. And he kept tripping over his own huge feet when they played tag. And in Red Rover no one ever dared him over. "This is no fun at all," Sammy said, scuffing off into the woods.

He sat down on a log and thought about crying. "Oh, why did I make that stupid wish?" Sammy said, kicking at a dead stump. "I'm too big to fit down my hole. And too big to play with my friends. Bigger is not better!" he yelled into the wind. "It's not better! It's not...."

"Sammy, Sammy! Wake up!"

Sammy opened his eyes and looked up into his mother's face. "Mama!"

"It got so late, I came looking for you. Little rabbits shouldn't be out after twilight."

"But I'm not little. I'm...." Sammy looked at the trees. They were gigantic again. He glanced at his reflection. A wide-eyed little rabbit stared back. "I'm not enormous anymore. It was all a dream. A terrible dream!"

"Come, Sammy. It's past your bedtime. Little rabbits need their sleep if they're going to grow up big and strong." Mama held out her paw to Sammy. "You do want to grow up to be a big rabbit, don't you?"

"Sure, someday," Sammy smiled. He looked up into the trees, their branches dancing back and forth in the magic wind. "But I think maybe I'm just the right size for now." And he said it loudly enough for all the hollow to hear.

A Closer Look

Did you ever find yourself in a group where you were the smallest one? How did it make you feel? Almost everything in nature starts out small and then grows. Giant oaks were once tiny acorns. Huge sunflowers began as slender seeds. And the biggest blocker in the National Football League started out as a wiggly little baby. Everyone grows at his own special pace. That's why some of your friends may be taller or bigger then you. But that doesn't mean you have to *feel* little. Being bigger doesn't make you a better person. It won't make you smarter or nicer. Remember Sammy's wish and the trouble it brought? Being just who you are is being the best you can be!

What's Next?

There's a special story in the Bible about how Jesus made a teeny, tiny man named Zacchaeus feel ten feet tall. Why not get your Bible and read about it in Luke 19:1–10? Then come back here and continue reading.

Now think of someone who is littler than you. Perhaps it's your sister or baby brother. It could be a cousin or next-door neighbor. Maybe it's the kindergarten girl at the bus stop. Is there something you can do to make that person *feel big*? Maybe they'd like to ride your bike or help you with a project. You could invite them over to share a bowl of popcorn and watch cartoons. Why not take them to one of your baseball games?

Whatever you decide to do, do it soon. Then you'll discover a secret—when you try to make other people feel big, *you* feel big, too!

☆ ☆ ☆

Fun Stuff

Old Abner has a message for you. But the magic wind has blown all the words into the pond! Can you help him find them? Look for the words hidden in the box of letters. Search forward, down and diagonal. Circle each word. We circled the first word for you. Then copy the words in order in the blanks below.

Message:

you	the
way	are
special	you
just	are

s	a	t	y	y	e	l
c	p	h	m	o	p	u
a	r	e	z	u	d	f
y	j	b	c	t	k	n
i	o	w	g	i	d	b
x	c	u	f	w	a	y
j	u	s	t	a	r	l
h	o	s	x	e	v

_____ _____ _____ _____

_____ _____ _____ _____ _____!

(See Answer Page.)

Those Amazing Animals!

In the animal world, some of the smallest animals are also the smartest. Even the Bible takes notice of this fact!

There are four things that are small but unusually wise:
Ants: *they aren't strong, but store up food for the winter.*
Cliff badgers: *delicate little animals who protect themselves by living among the rocks.*
Locusts: *though they have no leader, they stay together in swarms.*
Lizards: *they are easy to catch and kill, yet are found even in king's palaces!*

—Proverbs 30:24–28 (TLB)

Tell Me Another One

The world is filled with big and little things. Here are some of the most unusual:

The world's smallest Bible has pages half the size of a postage stamp. This tiny Bible was printed in Scotland in 1895. You *can* read it—if you have a strong magnifying glass!

The tallest twins are Michael and James Lanier. Their height reaches to a whopping seven feet four inches! The shortest twins are Doreen Williams and Darlene McGregor. Each of these ladies is only four feet one inch tall.

The largest animal is the blue bottom whale. And not only that—but it's the *female* blue bottom whale. It is also the fastest growing, reaching a weight of twenty-nine tons in less than two years. What's the slowest growing animal? It's the deep-sea clam of the North Atlantic. It takes this creature an estimated one hundred years to reach a length of less than one-third inch!

From Me to God

Sometimes I don't like the size I am, God. Whenever I feel that way, help me to remember that I'm Your special creation. I know now that good things come in all sizes!

Building a Better Me

How to Tell Someone You're Sorry

1. *Do it soon.* The longer you wait, the harder it is.

2. *Pray before you begin.* Perhaps a prayer like this:

   I'm scared, God. I know I should apologize, but it's so hard! Go before me and then go with me. Thanks!

God will help you, if you'll just ask Him.

3. *Keep your apology short.* A simple "I'm sorry" is usually best. Then you can know you've done the right thing, whatever the outcome.

All About Easter And Me

Christmas is always on December 25, right? And the Fourth of July is always on July 4. But Easter is on a different Sunday every year. It can come as early as March 22 or as late as April 25. Why? Because Easter is the first Sunday following the first full moon in the spring. So whatever day it falls on this year—celebrate! Happy Easter!

Start Here

It's Easter! A time to plan for soccer games and bike rides and fishing trips to the lake. It's a time to remember, too—the story of the disciples and Jesus, of Pilate and the soldiers, of that stone thrown aside by the power of God, and the risen Christ. Because even though those things happened a long time ago, they're a part of you this very minute. Really!

The Easter story gives you *hope*. For big things, like eternal life. And for the not-so-big things, too—like a better grade on your next spelling test. The Easter story gives you *love*. It shows you God likes you just the way you are—even if some of the other kids make fun of the way you draw or how you run relays or where you live. The Easter story gives you *joy*. You're part of God's family—and nobody has a better reason to smile...and laugh...maybe even giggle once in a while.

So come on. Let's be part of the Easter story. You can read a little each day during Easter week, or you can read it all at once. First you can see what happened long ago. Then try answering an Easter story riddle by filling in the blanks. And finally, read *Easter and Me* to find out why Easter was meant just for you! At the back, there's even a maze tucked in just for fun.

Happy Easter!

—Mary Lou Carney

The Easter Parade Begins...

The colt was brought to Jesus and the disciples threw their cloaks across its back for him to ride on. Then many in the crowd spread out their coats along the road before him, while others threw down leafy branches from the fields. He was in the center of the procession with crowds ahead and behind, and all of them shouting, . . . "Praise God for him who comes in the name of the Lord!"
—Mark 11:7–9 (TLB)

The air in Jerusalem vibrated with the sounds of shouting and laughter. A parade was coming! Jesus was riding on a donkey and His disciples were walking beside Him. Everyone along the way—mothers and fathers, aunts and uncles, kids with grins almost as wide as the dusty road on which they were standing—waved palm branches and shouted, "Hurray! Hosanna!" They threw their coats on the street to make a colorful path for the donkey's hooves....

???RIDDLE???

I stood there munching
Grass and hay
And bellowing out
An occasional bray.

Then two men came,
Took me away.
It turned out to be
An incredible day!

WHO AM I?

___   ___   ___   ___   ___   ___

Easter and Me

You can join the Easter parade, too. Can you think of any ways to praise Jesus this week? Maybe you'd like to tell a friend or someone close to you how special God is to you. Or you could sing a special song or psalm to Him. And right now you could even offer this prayer:

Jesus, You are my Friend.
Knowing that makes me very happy!

They Make Him Mad!

He [Jesus] went to the Temple and began to drive out the merchants and their customers, and knocked over the tables of the moneychangers and the stalls of those selling doves, and stopped everyone from bringing in loads of merchandise.
—Mark 11:15–16 (TLB)

Did you ever see someone do something that really made you mad, something that was so wrong you just wanted to stand up and say so? That's what happened to Jesus!

The Temple was very special to Him. It was His Father's house, a place set apart for worship and prayer. But merchants had seen the crowds that came to the Temple, and all they cared about was how much money they could make. So they set up their tables—right there in church—and sold things needed in Temple worship. The sounds of coins and bargaining were louder than the sounds of prayer. This made Jesus angry! Here's what He did. . . .

???RIDDLE???

He overturned the tables
Of all who bought and sold
He quoted holy scripture
Penned in days of old.

My tiny cage He shattered
And skyward I did fly.
My wings stretched out in freedom.

Now tell me, WHO AM I?

____ ____ ____ ____

Easter and Me

God's house is an extraordinary place! It's a place you come to be near your very Best Friend—to learn about Him and listen to Him.

On the line below write something you will do when you go to church this week to show God you know how special His house is. Will you be friendly and reverent? Listen quietly to the sermon? Not giggle, not whisper? What will you do?

An Expensive Present

Then Mary took a jar of costly perfume... and anointed Jesus'
feet with it and wiped them with her hair. And the house was
filled with fragrance. But Judas Iscariot, one of his disciples—
the one who would betray him—said, "That perfume was worth
a fortune."

—John 12:3–5 (TLB)

Has anyone ever given you a present? Maybe it was your birthday or Christmas. Or maybe it wasn't any special occasion. Perhaps they just wanted to give you something because they thought you were pretty special.

In Bethany, a small town near Jerusalem, lived a family that Jesus loved: Mary, her sister Martha, and her brother Lazarus. Because Jesus had just brought Lazarus back to life after he died, there was going to be a big dinner as a celebration. Mary wanted to show Jesus just how thankful she was and how much she loved Him. So while Jesus was at the dinner she brought him the most expensive thing she had....

???RIDDLE???

I had been in the jar forever.
(It was awfully stuffy and tight!)
I'd waited for days and months and years
For what would happen that night.

Mary held the jar so gently
As she walked down the narrow street.
I filled the room with a fragrance rare
When she poured me on Jesus' feet.

WHAT AM I?

_____ _____ _____ _____ _____ _____ _____

Easter and Me

You have something of value to give to Jesus. Do you know what it is? It's not your baseball card collection or your new bike or even the money in your bank. It's your*self*. Why not tell Him about your gift right now?

> *Dear Jesus, I want to be everything You want me to be. Take my heart. Use my life. I give them to You now as my gift. Amen.*

A Very Special Meal

While he [Jesus] was still speaking, Judas... arrived with a mob equipped with swords and clubs...Judas had told them, "You will know which one to arrest when I go over and greet (kiss) him. Then you can take him easily." So as soon as they arrived he walked up to Jesus. "Master!" he exclaimed, and embraced him with a great show of friendliness. Then the mob arrested Jesus and held him fast.

—Mark 14:43–46 (TLB)

Don't you sometimes like to eat with your friends—split an order of french fries, share a pizza, or even have your mom set an extra place at the table? Jesus liked to eat with His friends, the disciples, too. They had a very special meal together the night before Jesus was crucified. It was their "Last Supper."

But while they ate and talked together, some other things were going on outside. The powerful religious leaders of the day, the Pharisees and Scribes, were busy plotting to kill Jesus. They were jealous because all the people listened to Him instead of them. They had even found one of Jesus' disciples who would help them. . . .

??? RIDDLE ???

I'm a symbol of love and affection
Given to those you hold dear.
Grandmas and grandpas and uncles,
Cousins from far and near.

But Judas, the evildoer,
Used me a different way
That night in the darkened garden
When he the Savior betrayed.

WHAT AM I?

A ____ ____ ____ ____

Easter and Me

It's not always easy to do what's right. It wasn't even easy for the Son of God! One of the things that gave Jesus strength to do what He knew must be done was prayer.

Did you know you can pray about anything—anywhere, anytime? Like the miserable day you spent in bed with the flu or that baseball game when you struck out. You can pray about good things, too, like fun vacations and healthy pets.

Why not try it right now? *Dear Jesus....*

✛   ✛   ✛

Crucify Him!

The chief priests and religious leaders were also standing around joking about Jesus.... and even the two robbers dying with him, cursed him.... Then Jesus called out with a loud voice,... "My God, my God, why have you deserted me?"... Then Jesus uttered another loud cry, and dismissed his spirit.
—Mark 15:31, 32b, 34, 37 (TLB)

Have you ever been so lonely that you felt you were the only person on the whole earth? That nobody cared about you at all? That's how lonely Christ was on Good Friday. The Jewish leaders were so afraid of Him that they persuaded Pilate, the governor, to order Him crucified. The Roman soldiers beat Him like a criminal and, finally, killed Him....

Easter and Me

Good Friday was the darkest day in all the history of the world. It wasn't just dark the way cloudy or stormy days are. It was dark because Christ took all our sin on Him. Because He alone took all our blame, setting us free to enjoy life. That's how much He loved us! Why not take a few minutes right now to thank Him?

*Dear Jesus, I want to learn to love You as much
as You love me. Thanks for everything! Amen.*

Sealing The Grave

The next day... the chief priests and Pharisees went to Pilate, and told him, ... "We request an order from you sealing the tomb until the third day, to prevent his disciples from coming and stealing his body and then telling everyone he came back to life! If that happens we'll be worse off than we were at first."... So they sealed the stone and posted guards to protect it.

—Matthew 27: 62, 64, 66 (TLB)

Don't you hate waiting? For your mom to finish grocery shopping or for those last minutes to pass before recess? Jesus' friends hated to wait, too—but they had to.

There had been no time for the proper burial rites for Jesus. His friend, Joseph of Arimathea, laid His body in a cave, then had a huge stone rolled in front of its entrance. Jesus' friends waited for the Sabbath to end so they could go to His grave and complete the burial rites.

But the leaders who had plotted against Jesus were worried. What if His disciples stole the body and claimed He had been raised from the dead? They decided to make sure this couldn't happen....

???RIDDLE???

The whole situation bothered me,
From the moment I saw His face.
Many were much too eager
To bring about His disgrace.

And even now, when He is dead,
I fear the consent I gave.
So I'm sending out Roman Soldiers
To guard this Jesus' grave.

WHO AM I?

____ ___ ___ ___ ____ ___

Easter and Me

The people who caused Christ's death were feeling guilty—and afraid. But they weren't sorry for what they'd done. Have you ever done something you shouldn't have—and then felt guilty about it later? That's because your *conscience* was bothering you. A conscience is God's special way of telling you when you've done wrong. Everybody makes mistakes; everyone needs to be forgiven. And God is always ready, waiting to pardon and love us. Is there something you need to be forgiven for? Why not ask God right now?

Dear God, I'm sorry for _____ .
Forgive me. With Your help, I'll do better. Thanks!

❖　❖　❖

A Happy Ending!

Suddenly there was a great earthquake; for an angel of the Lord came down from heaven and rolled aside the stone and sat on it. His face shone like lightning and his clothing was a brilliant white. The guards shook with fear when they saw him... Then the angel spoke to the women. "Don't be frightened!" he said. "I know you are looking for Jesus, who was crucified, but he isn't here! For he has come back to life again, just as he said he would."... The women ran from the tomb... filled with joy.
—Matthew 28: 2–6, 8 (TLB)

Don't you love a happy ending, one where the hero finally defeats all his enemies? Me, too! And the Easter story has one of the happiest endings of all time.

How sad the disciples and Jesus' other followers felt after His death. Was this the end of all the miracles? Were Jesus' teachings just words after all? Then came Sunday, the first day of the Jewish week. The women who had stood by Jesus at the cross now came to the tomb, determined to give His body the proper burial rites. But what a surprise they found....

???RIDDLE???

His enemies
Thought they'd won
When they used me to seal
The tomb of God's Son.

But three days later,
With bright lights and clatter,
God rolled me aside
And settled the matter!

WHAT AM I?

A ____ ____ ____ ____ ____

Easter and Me

Sometimes it's hard to believe that God is in control—especially when you don't get the things you want. But God cares about everything. He's watching over you all the time, no matter where you are. And He's busy planning lots of happy times and good things for you, too—birthday parties and best friends, sleep-overs and bike rides, pen-pal letters and unexpected surprises. But best of all, His love and Spirit are living in you. Everyday.

That's why Easter was meant just for *you*!

The women are on their way to Jesus' tomb—
but they're having trouble finding the right road.
Can you help them?

Answer Page

Answer to puzzle on page 16.

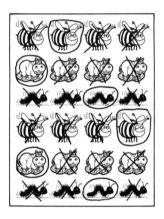

Page 24   It's fun to try new things!

Page 32   ASTRONAUT

Page 40   God will help you always!
           (See diagram.)

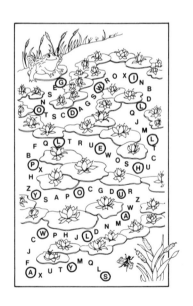

Page 41   Frogs

Page 60 (See diagram.)

Page 67 Down: 1. Valentine 2. Card 3. Red
Across: 2. Candy 4. Arrow 5. Love 6. Kind
7. Heart

Page 68 14 hearts

Page 76 Always Be Honest

Page 87 Yes

Page 97 Trust in the Lord and do good....

Page 114 Forgive

Page 122 You are special just the way you are! (See diagram.)

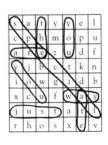

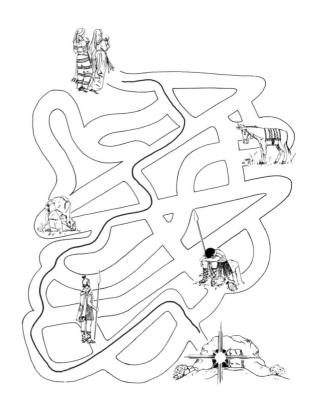